Cambridge checkpoint

Cambridge Assessment
International Education
Endorsed for learner support

Lower Secondary
World English
WORKBOOK

9

Monica Menon
Richa Ahuja
Belinda Danker
EDUCATIONAL CONSULTANT:
Sioban Parker

Registered Cambridge International Schools benefit from high-quality programmes, assessments and a wide range of support so that teachers can effectively deliver Cambridge Lower Secondary. Visit www.cambridgeinternational.org/lowersecondary to find out more.

Answers have been written by the authors. These may not fully reflect the approach of Cambridge Assessment International Education.

Answers are free to download at www.hoddereducation.com/cambridgeextras

Every effort has been made to trace all copyright holders, but if any have been inadvertently overlooked, the Publishers will be pleased to make the necessary arrangements at the first opportunity.

Although every effort has been made to ensure that website addresses are correct at time of going to press, Hodder Education cannot be held responsible for the content of any website mentioned in this book. It is sometimes possible to find a relocated web page by typing in the address of the home page for a website in the URL window of your browser.

Hachette UK's policy is to use papers that are natural, renewable and recyclable products and made from wood grown in well-managed forests and other controlled sources. The logging and manufacturing processes are expected to conform to the environmental regulations of the country of origin.

Orders: please contact Hachette UK Distribution, Hely Hutchinson Centre, Milton Road, Didcot, Oxfordshire OX11 7HH. Telephone: +44 (0)1235 827827. Email: education@hachette.co.uk Lines are open from 9 a.m. to 5 p.m., Monday to Friday. You can also order through our website: www.hoddereducation.com

ISBN: 978 1 398311404

© Monica Menon, Richa Ahuja and Belinda Danker 2021

First published in 2021 by

Hodder Education
An Hachette UK Company
Carmelite House
50 Victoria Embankment
London EC4Y 0DZ

www.hoddereducation.com

Impression number 10 9 8 7 6 5 4 3 2 1

Year 2025 2024 2023 2022 2021

Cover © Gianfranco Bella – stock.adobe.com

Typeset in FS Albert Light 12/14pt by DC Graphic Design Limited, Hextable, Kent.

Printed in the UK

A catalogue record for this title is available from the British Library.

Contents

Introduction   4

Unit 1	Making a stand	5
Unit 2	Travelling the world	13
Unit 3	Well-being	23
Unit 4	Food for the future	34
Unit 5	Technology matters	39
Unit 6	Instant fame	51
Unit 7	Space travel	60
Unit 8	Rules protect us … don't they?	71
Unit 9	Dreams and ambitions	83

Introduction

Welcome to *Cambridge Checkpoint Lower Secondary World English Workbook 9*. This is the third of three books intended to provide practice in the skills you have acquired by using the Cambridge Checkpoint Lower Secondary World English series of student's books. Each of the workbooks is planned to complement the corresponding student's book and to support the material contained in it.

The chapters in Workbook 9 reflect the topics contained in Student's Book 9. Each chapter contains exercises to allow you to practise a range of key skills in the use of English which, in general, follow the sequence of the advice given on these key skills in Student's Book 9.

This workbook is intended both to help you acquire the skills to be fully competent in your ability to understand and write English and also to act as valuable support in your preparation for the Cambridge Lower Secondary Checkpoint tests that you may take during your school career. There is no set way to approach using the workbook – you may wish to use it to supplement your understanding as you work through each chapter of the student's book or you may prefer to use it to recap on particular topics at a later point. It is hoped that the organisation of the material in the book is sufficiently flexible to allow whichever approach is best suited to your needs. You should write your answers in the space provided and should use additional paper if you need extra space.

Making a stand

Future tense or future continuous tense

Exercise 1

Choose the appropriate tense and fill in the blanks.

1   Once we reach home, we .... (will be watching / will watch) a documentary on Marley Dias.

2   Beginning next week, Robert .... (will film / will be filming) a movie about Kelvin Doe.

3   The train .... (will leave / will be leaving) at 11.45 a.m. sharp.

4   We .... (will be meeting / will meet) the engineer now.

5   Who .... (will be attending / will attend) the conference this year?

6   She .... (will be travelling / will travel) around the world for the next few years.

7   You .... (will contact / will be contacting) that supplier tomorrow.

8   I .... (will shop / will be shopping) for parts to build my battery before our meeting.

9   At the end of this semester, the school .... (will be testing / will test) them on the topics learned.

10 I .... (will be completing / will complete) my homework on time.

Past tense sentences

Exercise 2a

Choose an appropriate word from the box. Change the word to the past tense and fill in the blanks.

buy	invite	organise	speak	meet
enjoy	use	manage	collect	donate

1 He .... scrap metal to build his battery.

2 The team .... supplies cheaply.

3 How many of you .... watching the documentary on Kelvin Doe?

4 The governor .... them to visit him.

5 Bye Bye Plastics .... the clean-up campaigns for Bali's beaches.

6 They .... to get 6000 signatures for their petition.

7 'Little Miss Flint' .... to the President face to face.

8 The President .... her when he visited her hometown.

9 She .... her collection of books to the poor schools.

10 Marley .... many books to donate to the school in Jamaica.

Past tense passage

Exercise 2b

Fill in the blanks by changing the verb in brackets into the past tense.

Have you ever .... (wonder) how people in the past .... (go)

about starting a protest? They .... (use) signboards, ... (stand)

in groups or .... (walk) around in circles and .... (chant),

holding their homemade signboards in the air. After the era of the Great Depression, many people

.... (are) without jobs and no money to feed themselves and their families.

They .... (voice) their unhappiness and anger in the hopes that the government

.... (will) do something to help them. It .... (is) a time of

unrest and uncertainty.

Present perfect continuous tense

Exercise 3

Choose an appropriate word for each sentence and fill in the blanks using the present perfect continuous tense.

fix	donate	study	collect	jog
use	write	build	ask	grow

1 I am panting because I .... in the park for my evening exercise.

2 I .... in a university in Canada for six months.

3 My factory .... generators that are broken since we started this business.

4 Marley .... books to reach her goal of 1000 books to donate.

5 She .... clothes and books to the poor around the world for the past 10 years.

6 He .... batteries since he was 11 years old.

7 You .... scrap metals to build generators for a long time.

8 Bye Bye Plastics .... in popularity since they started the campaign when they were teenagers.

9 They .... to the governor every year to ask for help.

10 We .... for help to solve the problem since it began.

Words as nouns and verbs

Exercise 4

Choose the option that correctly describes the noun or verb shown.

1 call (noun)

   a That phone call was to inform us that the protest is about to begin.

   b Will you call the others to inform them that the protest is about to begin?

2 sign (verb)

    a The government agreed to sign the document to meet the protesters' demands.

    b The government agreeing to the protesters' demands is a huge sign of better things to come for the townspeople.

3 watch (verb)

    a He kept looking at his watch because he did not want to be late for the president's speech on television.

    b They were made to watch the president's speech on saving the environment

4 bank (noun)

    a Make sure you bank all the donations you received to support your campaign.

    b They had to go to the bank to deposit the donations they received in support of their campaign.

5 move (noun)

    a Their move to a bigger office was to house more people involved in the campaign.

    b They want to move into a bigger office because of the increased number of people involved in the campaign.

6 permit (verb)

    a You will need a permit before you are allowed to carry out a protest march.

    b I wonder if the government will permit you to carry out a protest march.

7 insult (verb)

    a The department chief heard the insult made by his employee about his ability to lead the campaign.

    b The department knew that his employee did not mean to insult him.

8 present (noun)

    a He received a present after he delivered his speech to the townspeople to assure them that good changes were coming.

    b He had to present his speech to the townspeople to assure them that good changes were coming.

9 impact (verb)

    a The impact of the constant protesting resulted in changes.

    b The constant protesting was to impact the government for change to happen.

10 protest (verb)

    a They all wanted to join hands in a line as a peaceful way to protest.

    b Their protest was peaceful as they joined hands and stood without disbanding.

Noun or verb?

Exercise 5

Decide which of the underlined words is a noun or a verb and place a tick in the appropriate column.

Sentence	Noun (✔)	Verb (✔)
Use the <u>paste</u> to stick up your slogan for the protest march.		
<u>Paste</u> the paper with your handwritten slogan on the signboard.		
Make sure you <u>pay</u> for the meals for your volunteers for the campaign event.		
They all received their <u>pay</u> for working on the campaign.		
Please turn the <u>light</u> off because I do not want anyone to see what we are doing for our protest march.		
She had to <u>light</u> up the signboard as they continued protesting into the night.		
You should use the <u>drill</u> to get everyone ready to place the campaign posters onto the walls in the lobby.		
Make sure you <u>drill</u> the holes in the right places to hold the campaign posters.		
You need to <u>back</u> me up during the meeting with the governor about our demands for a bigger environmental budget.		
My <u>back</u> hurts from sitting in the meeting with the governor about our demands for a bigger environmental budget.		
The <u>answer</u> that you gave about what we stand for is incorrect.		
You do not have to <u>answer</u> questions if you are unsure of our reasons for the cause.		
We need to stand up for changes in the medical <u>care</u> system in our city.		
We have to <u>care</u> for the volunteers who help us fight our cause.		
I need to take a <u>break</u> from this campaign.		
Do not <u>break</u> any of the signboards that we need for this campaign.		
Can you help <u>blow</u> up those balloons with the slogans on, please?		
It was a big <u>blow</u> to me when the suppliers delivered the balloons with spelling errors in the slogans.		
Change the cushion <u>cover</u> for the one that has our logo, so people know about our cause.		
<u>Cover</u> the windows with posters about our campaign.		

Same sound

Exercise 6

Fill in the blanks with the appropriate words from the words provided in the brackets.

1   His .... grew up to be an activist for the farmers and had to work in the
    .... all day to show his support for them. (sun / son)

2   The .... of money will pay for .... of our campaign
    expenses. (some / sum)

3   The folk .... from France is about how people who stood for a cause used a
    mouse with a long .... as their mascot. (tail / tale)

4   You can use .... to build a generator but make sure you lock it away so that
    people do not .... it. (steal / steel)

5   Farmers carried out a protest because they could not buy seed to .... and their
    wives could not buy cloth to .... clothes for themselves. (sew / sow)

6   .... bus ride to town for the beach clean-up takes about an
    .... (our / hour)

7   It will take a long time for that blister on your .... to ....
    because you walked a long way in the protest march. (heel / heal)

8   How much is the bus .... to the annual .... where the
    governor will speak about the environment? (fare / fair)

9   The people who collect the .... at the campaign event will wear a red sash
    around their .... (waist / waste)

10 She would like to know the best .... to .... the rubbish
    discarded by irresponsible tourists. (way / weigh)

Passive voice

Exercise 7

Change the sentences to the passive voice without including the do-er. (Remember to change the word order.)

1 The council will replace the old pipes with new ones.

....

....

2 Petitioners will help with the campaign by obtaining signatures.

....

....

3 The bus company will transport activists to the capital city.

....

....

4 The water company will donate crates of bottled water.

....

....

5 The president will visit the people of the town.

....

....

6 Villagers will protest for the lack of fresh water.

....

....

7 The young protester will visit the governor.

....

....

8 We will bring this up with the government.

....

....

9 The dam will break if nothing is done.

....

....

10 The people will demand change.

....

....

Travelling the world

Prefixes and suffixes

Exercise 1

Use appropriate prefixes (dis-, in-, un-, over-) or appropriate suffixes (-less, -able, -ible, -ment) for the words below. Some words may use prefixes and suffixes in the same word and some root words may have different prefixes and suffixes.

The first one has been done for you.

Word	Prefix	Suffix
1 pleasure	displeasure	pleasurable
2 appropriate		
3 agree		
4 comfort		
5 reverse		
6 obey		
7 appear		
8 tire		
9 heat		
10 name		
11 merry		
12 move		

5W1H

Exercise 2

Describe a holiday you have been on or describe a holiday you would like to go on. You may like to attach a photograph of your holiday, or a picture of a similar holiday, to this page.

Where did you go?	
Who did you go with?	
When did you go?	
Why did you decide to go to this place?	
What did you do there?	
How did you get around?	

Passive voice 1

Exercise 3a

Fill in the blanks by changing the words in brackets into the passive voice.

1 It is common for wildlife to .... (protect) by the locals.

2 The land .... (maintain) with government funds.

3 The Eiffel Tower .... (visit) by thousands of tourists.

4 Coral of the Great Barrier Reef is .... (damage) by divers.

5 Revenue .... (generate) by tourists who visit the country.

6 The wealth of a country .... (increase) by tourism.

7 Damage to the land and wildlife .... (create) by over-tourism.

8 Frustration .... (cause) by long queues to visit the country's attraction.

9 Tourists .... (help) by information in brochures.

10 The ruins are .... (clean) up by the authorities.

Passive voice 2

Exercise 3b

Underline the passive voice in the passage below.

It is common that irresponsible behaviour towards the environment and wildlife are not being addressed by governments overseas. Without this, how then do governments protect their environment and wildlife? I believe that awareness should be created through education and rules should be enforced. Fines should be imposed any time the rules are not followed. Information about these measures should be included in tourist brochures. This message should be appreciated by tourists and a serious view of inconsiderate and irresponsible behaviours should be taken by those in charge. The message that the land and wildlife are precious and protected should be clearly communicated so it can be understood by tourists.

Laying down the law is one thing, but how much of this is enforced in relation to tourists? To implement and enforce these kinds of rules involves a skilled workforce which may not be available in poorer nations. Time and money are needed to train the right people for this work. Decisions have to be made by governments about which areas money should be spent on. This leaves governments with dilemmas on how to manage the country's funds. Does this then mean that global assistance should be available to poorer nations to help fight pollution and damage caused by over-tourism?

Passive to active voice

Exercise 4

The following sentences are written in the passive voice. Convert them to the active voice.

1 A sense of peace is given by the formations of sand dunes in deserts.

....

....

2 Guides will be hired for your visit to see the turtles.

....

....

3 Information is sent out in advance for many places visited by tourists.

    ....

    ....

4 They will not be held responsible if you step off the pathways.

    ....

    ....

5 Touching any flora is not recommended, as they are poisonous.

    ....

    ....

6 Those who litter will be heavily fined.

    ....

    ....

7 Turtles will have to be protected from visitors.

    ....

    ....

8 The government makes sure that the environment and wildlife are protected.

    ....

    ....

9 $1000 has to be paid by tourists for a permit to see the lowland gorillas.

    ....

    ....

10 The Lost City is hidden deep in the jungles of Colombia.

....

....

Modals

Exercise 5

Identify the purpose of the modal verb used in the sentences below and write this in the space in the brackets.

Choose from these options in the box.

advice	question	permission	obligation	speculation
doubt	opinion	ability	deduction about past actions	

For example:
- We should pay a fee. (advice)
- Should we pay a fee? (question)
- We must pay a fee. (obligation)

1 May I visit the Eiffel Tower, please? (...)

2 I must pay attention to the details in the brochure. (...)

3 We should be careful not to disturb the habitats of the wildlife there. (...)

4 The government of Rwanda must charge a high price for the permit to see the lowland gorillas.

(...)

5 Divers who swim to see the Great Barrier Reef may have caused damage to the coral.

(...)

6 Do you remember what we should not do when visiting that country? (...)

7 They could have made a mistake about the laws of Paris. (...)

8 Professor Green believes that over-tourism might have caused much damage to countries around

the world. (...)

9 Wildlife on the Galapagos Islands must be protected as they have some unique animals not

found anywhere else in the world. (...)

10 Irresponsible and inconsiderate tourists must be punished. (...)

Writing instructions

Exercise 6

Use modals to expand on the steps provided on how to pack for a camping trip and how to behave while you are on your trip. An example is provided for you. Remember, not everything is compulsory.

Example:

Packing for the trip	
Step 1: Clothes	You should pack: a hat, sunglasses, long trousers and long-sleeved shirt, swimsuit.
Step 2: Food and drink	
Step 3: Personal items	
Step 4: Tools	
Step 5: Medication	
At the campsite	
Step 1: Setting up	
Step 2: Check out the area	
Step 3: Check the facilities	
Step 4: Rules of the area	

Vocabulary and sentences

Exercise 7

Find the meaning of each word and write it in the middle column. Then, create a sentence using each word and write it in the right-hand column.

Word	Meaning	Sentence
caravan		
journey		
traveller		
pilgrim		
commerce		
accommodate		
merchant		
merchandise		
conservation		
diverse		

Nouns to noun phrases

Exercise 8

Convert the underlined nouns in each sentence into noun phrases.

1 The slope consisted of <u>terraces</u> carved into the mountainside.

....

....

2 You should not steal <u>things</u>.

....

....

3 We should respect the <u>environment</u>.

....

....

4 Locals usually protect their <u>land and wildlife</u>.

....

....

5 We visited the <u>Eiffel Tower</u> in Paris last spring.

....

....

6 We should all be careful not to disturb the <u>wildlife</u>.

....

....

7 Tourists sometimes cause <u>damage</u> when they visit other countries.

....

....

8 I looked down and marvelled at the <u>site</u> below.

....

....

9 The <u>size</u> of the group was nothing compared to the thousands of <u>tourists</u>.

....

....

10 Although it was a challenge, it made the <u>journey</u> a rewarding one.

....

....

Compound nouns

Exercise 9

Use the definitions from the box to form appropriate compound nouns, using the clues given in the sentences.

table	vine	yard	motor	story
sun	storm	ship	air	sky
port	friend	police	back	cycle
dining	thunder	rise	officer	scraper

1 Place where grapes are grown ....

2 Piece of furniture used at home when you have meals ....

3 A form of transport. ....

4 You see this early in the morning. ....

5 Place to board a plane to travel overseas. ....

6 A tall building. ....

7 Related to stormy weather. ....

8 The history behind a story. ....

9 Enforces the law. ....

10 A relationship between two people. ....

Fact or opinion?

Exercise 10

Read the sentences and tick to indicate whether they are fact or opinion.

	Fact (✔)	Opinion (✔)
1 Cuidad Perdita is hidden deep in the jungles of Colombia.		
2 The trek up the mountain may be difficult.		
3 She thinks the Eiffel Tower is the most visited tourist attraction in the world.		
4 He claims that tourists visit the Galapagos Islands all the time.		
5 I believe that everyone loves to visit Paris.		
6 Deserts have extreme temperatures.		
7 Someone commented that only people who love nature will take eco-trips.		
8 The huge orange sand dunes gave me a feeling of peace.		
9 The Fenyan Ecolodge employs local Bedouin people.		
10 A caravanserai is a building that looks square on the outside.		

3 Well-being

Imperative verbs

Exercise 1

Fill in the blanks with the appropriate imperative verb from the box.

Pass	Play	Think	Get	Pack
Keep	Step	Stretch	Balance	Bend
Take	Hold	Relax	Complete	Jump

1 .... ready for basketball practice.

2 .... your bag now or you will be late for the gym.

3 .... on one leg.

4 .... fit!

5 .... your knees when lifting weights or you will hurt your back.

6 .... the back of your legs or you will pull a muscle.

7 .... the ball to your team-mate.

8 .... aside to give the yoga instructor some room to move.

9 .... fairly, do not cheat.

10 .... about your next move before you throw the ball.

11 .... your vitamins now!

12 .... your homework now or you cannot go out to cycle.

13 .... your breath underwater for as long as you can.

14 .... higher for the ball, don't be lazy.

15 .... your muscles or you will suffer from cramps.

Compound adjectives 1

Exercise 2a

Fill in the blanks with the appropriate compound adjective from the box.

| world-famous | well-recognised | time-saving | 30-minute | most-followed |
| record-breaking | English-speaking | well-respected | part-time | mouth-watering |

1 Although the yoga centre is in Italy, it has .... instructors for those who cannot understand Italian.

2 The meditation teacher wants to convert from teaching .... to full-time at the centre.

3 He is a fitness coach who writes ...., healthy recipes, which are delicious.

4 Jamila is ....! Everyone from all over the world knows who she is and what she does.

5 The Olympic swimmer swam the length of the pool in .... time.

6 You should try out the online .... workout that is free of charge.

7 He is so .... that people from other countries can tell who he is when they see him.

8 The yoga teacher is so .... that her students admire her and think highly of her.

9 Tony's .... solution to exercising online saves you hours in travelling to the gym and back again.

10 She is among the .... on Instagram and Facebook for her exercise routines.

Compound adjectives 2

Exercise 2b

Pair the words in the box to form compound adjectives. Some words may be used more than once.

well	highly	time	world
regarded	saving	known	rested
respected	famous	adjusted	

....

....

....

....

Intensifying adjectives

Exercise 3

Fill in the blanks with adjectives from the box to intensify the sentences.

most	especially	particularly	utterly	exceptionally
extremely	big	great	large	highly

1 Jonathan's win in athletics in record-breaking time was a .... event for his country.

2 He did .... well in his examinations this year compared to last year.

3 Even though the yoga centre charged high fees, it had an unusually .... number of people who signed up for classes.

4 It was an .... hot day for the runners in the long-distance competition.

5 She received the .... support from the Sports Council for her participation in the national championships.

6 John was .... concerned about the management of the fitness club as they are doing things differently.

7 His plan to enter the National Track and Field Championships sounds like a good one, ... since he said he needed to exercise regularly.

8 It is .... unlikely that Mary will agree to your suggestion because she has other plans.

9 It was a .... achievement for him when he was nominated the fittest competitor in his age group.

10 I am .... disappointed with your performance at the last fitness competition because you did not have enough discipline to practice.

Spelling rules

Exercise 4
Convert the verb in brackets and fill in the blanks. Remember to check the spelling of the words when '-ing' is added.

1 This fitness coach is .... (bore).

2 His trainees have commented that his training techniques are .... (tire).

3 James likes attending yoga lessons with Ms Betty as she is .... (amuse).

4 That was a .... (surprise) result. I did not expect that to happen.

5 It was, indeed, ... (excite) to receive news that my son qualified for the track and field finals.

6 In spite of his determination and practice, the results were .... (frustrate).

7 As she doesn't speak his language well, she found the coach's instructions .... (confuse).

8 He found it .... (puzzle) that they did not select him for the community fitness event.

9 Gwen finds one of her students .... (irritate) as he keeps fidgeting during their meditation sessions.

10 'Oh wow! You have made .... (amaze) changes in your life!'

All kinds of adjectives

Exercise 5

Fill in the blanks with the most appropriate adjective from the box.

extremely	tiring	twice as many	strong-willed	astonishing
fast-moving	well-recognised	best	confusing	amazing

1 The .... traffic was a good thing because everyone could get to the games on time.

2 It was .... painful to hear that I missed the first place by a mere second.

3 The whole week of exercising turned out to be a .... one.

4 She showed .... drive, determination and discipline to reach her goals of staying healthy in spite of all her medical issues.

5 The fitness coach is .... all over the world for his innovative and revolutionary way of training.

6 In one year, this new yoga instructor had .... students as the instructor who joined the centre two years ago.

7 In spite of his physical disability, this young man is .... and determined to use his legs again.

8 I find the determination of some athletes ....

9 It must be .... for some to understand how the mind can hold so much information and functions.

10 Winning the yoga competition was the .... thing that happened to her.

Rephrase the sentence

Exercise 6

Rephrase the sentences by creating compound adjectives where applicable.

1 Many people know this fitness coach well because of his online videos.

....

....

2 The workout that lasts 30 minutes is very popular among the participants.

....

....

3 All the recipes in her cookbook are so delicious that they make your mouth water.

....

....

4 The yoga student teaches only part time on weekends because she has a full-time job.

....

....

5 The trainer is known widely because he is organised in how he trains.

....

....

6 Not many athletes have broken records in their performances at major sporting events.

....

....

7 All it takes for you to feel rejuvenated is five minutes in a meditation session.

....

....

8 He has brought up some ideas about how to run a fitness programme that provokes thinking.

....

....

9 The head of the fitness centre is respected highly as he takes a lot of interest in people who are keen to keep fit.

....

....

10 To look healthy takes a lot of exercise, balanced meals and sufficient rest.

....

....

Comparisons

Exercise 7a

Fill in the blanks with appropriate adjectives from the box. You may use the same words more than once.

as good as	best	half as much
better	twice as much	all the more important

1 With all that is going on among the trainees, it is .... that you focus on exercising regularly.

2 She is .... anyone else in the team, if not better.

3 We have to acknowledge that some are .... than others in their fitness levels.

4 The twins have to eat .... healthy food than their classmates.

5 According to the doctor, the couple need to consume fewer carbohydrates so they have to eat
.... rice as they usually do.

6 The .... routine for her is exercise and meditation every day,
if possible.

7 A balanced meal, exercise and sufficient sleep give the ....
combination for a healthy life.

8 She will have .... health if she pays attention to what she eats.

9 We should always be mindful to eat .... as we need to stay
strong and healthy.

10 He knew he had to exercise .... if he wanted to beat the
champion in the track and field championships.

Using comparisons

Exercise 7b
Fill in the blanks with the appropriate comparative phrase.

as good as	best	half as much
better	twice as much	all the more important

James is a true sportsman in field events. He spends .... time as his
team-mates practising his long jumps in field events because he feels he needs more training. He
constantly feels like he needs to be .... if not ....
.... than his idol, his brother, who had won the bronze medal in the 2016 Olympic Games.

His mother would always say that James strives to be the ....
that he can be even if he knows he has met the expectations of his coach. He spends
.... time watching television or lounging around as he does practising
and training. When weather prevents him from training, it becomes ....
that he doubles up his practice after.

Comprehension skills

Exercise 8a

Answer the questions based on the article 'Mindfulness' on page 44 of the Student's Book.

1 According to the article, what is mindfulness?

....

....

2 How can learning mindfulness help us? Name two ways.

....

....

3 Name three ways you can develop mindfulness. How will these benefit you?

....

....

4 Why do you think most people pay attention to what is wrong in their lives?

....

....

5 After reading the article, describe one way you will develop and practise mindfulness in your life.

....

....

Summarising

Exercise 8b

Write a summary of about 100 words of the article 'Mindfulness' on page 44 of the Student's Book to check your understanding of the topic.

....

....

....

....

....

....

....

Phrasal verbs

Exercise 9

Underline the most appropriate phrasal verb in the sentences below.

1   He (dropped out of / kept leaving) the national fitness team because of problems at home.

2   It is sometimes difficult to (share something with / get along with) others who have different goals from you.

3   Barney (got away with / got something from) cheating in the race.

4   The yoga centre had to (call off / bring up) the grand opening event because of the weather.

5   The fitness centre is (giving away / handing up) free memberships to promote the opening of their new premises.

6   You need to (complete out / fill out) an application form before you can join as a member.

7   We need to (find out / look out) more information before we join their fitness classes.

8   Make sure you do not (leave out / leave in) any details on the application form when joining the meditation classes.

9   Be wise in (choosing out / picking out) the best instructor to train you at the gym.

10 You need to (put off / put on) suitable clothing when exercising to ensure it does not restrict your movement.

Comprehension

Exercise 10

Read the article 'Teenage risk-taking – the positive side' on page 48 of the Student's Book, then answer the questions below.

1 What do you think the writer means by 'more complex tasks'?

....

....

....

2 Which word tells you that it is the opinion of the government that people are mature by the age of 18?

....

....

....

3 Do you think the writer believes that being impulsive and taking risks are generally a bad thing which teenagers should be discouraged from doing? Give two sentences that support your answer.

....

....

....

4 State one sentence in the article that is an opinion of the writer. Why do you say so?

....

....

....

4 Food for the future

Present perfect tense 1

Exercise 1

Fill in the blanks with the present perfect tense of the verbs in brackets.

1 I .... (learn) to cook.

2 We .... (ask) for a table on the terrace in the Italian restaurant.

3 They .... not .... (try) Swedish food before.

4 .... you .... (roast) turkey for
Christmas before?

5 She .... not .... (taste) roasted crickets ever!

6 I .... (bake) earthworms as a snack if you are hungry.

7 .... you .... (tell) the rest of our class
about the noodle party?

8 How .... you .... (prepare) the leg of lamb?

9 We .... (eat) all the chocolates because they were more
inviting than fried grasshoppers.

10 The guests .... always .... (enjoy) food
made by the host who is a chef.

Present perfect tense 2

Exercise 2

Fill in the blanks with the appropriate verb.

People's tastes in the kind of food they eat .... (has / have) (evolve) over
time. I .... (has / have) (come) to accept eating meat and seafood as
normal. Over time, people .... (has / have) (become) more daring in the
kind of food they are willing to try.

I .... (has / have) (hear) stories of how delicious unusual food can be.

More recently, food such as grasshoppers, earthworms and crickets ....

(has / have) (become) the 'in-thing'. It .... (has / have) (make) me wonder

about what these taste like, but I .... (has / have) not .... (find)

the courage to try them. I .... (has / have) (convince) myself that they

must be as yucky as they look!

Present perfect passive voice

Exercise 3

Convert the following sentences into the present perfect passive form without including the do-er.

For example:
- They will increase the intake of carbohydrates. (active)
- The intake of carbohydrates has increased. (passive)

1 The caterers will include vegetables in every dish.

....

2 They will increase yoga fees.

....

3 Management built the meditation centre on a hill.

....

4 People make fishcakes from fresh fish.

....

5 Someone cooks nutritious food in this centre every day.

....

6 Her guests do not like the dishes with insects in them.

....

7 They import prawns from Australia.

....

8 The factories make cheese from milk taken from dairy cows.

....

9 They export lamb from New Zealand.

....

10 The shop sells interesting snacks with crickets.

....

Dependent prepositions 1

Exercise 4a

Fill in the blanks with an appropriate preposition from the box.

about	to	in	at	from
of	behind	on	with	between

1 My choice of food depends .... what is available in this café.

2 Sheila and I always have arguments .... each other about who will pay for dinner.

3 Please ring the restaurant to ask .... their specials today.

4 Find a table .... the wall at the restaurant so no one can see what we have ordered.

5 There is an arrangement .... us that we will take turns to cook dinner.

6 We were asked .... roast the chicken instead of deep frying it.

7 The guests looked .... the host appreciatively as all the delicious food appeared.

8 Please think .... your brother and do not finish all the food yourself.

9 The newly graduated chefs specialise .... insect soup, which is believed to provide essential proteins.

10 The caterer has to travel .... one end of the city to the other to deliver food.

Dependent prepositions 2

Exercise 4b

Fill in the blanks with an appropriate preposition.

1 What do you think .... the food here?

2 We need to look .... how the chefs are cooking the meats.

3 The judges have to base their decisions .... which dish is the tastiest.

4 Let us watch the documentary .... how food was traditionally prepared in India.

5 Please take the cheese .... the pantry cupboard.

6 I have to decide .... a seafood or vegetarian dinner.

7 The bottles of juice are .... the kitchen.

8 We should visit that new restaurant .... James and his cousin.

9 How long do you think it would take .... get to the food court by bus?

10 I have a preference .... seafood instead of meat.

Identifying grammar

Exercise 5

Read the article below that is from page 62 of the Student Book. There are two parts to this exercise.

Part A

Highlight the active voice.

Underline the passive voice.

Scientists across the world, from Amsterdam to Adelaide, have been hard at work developing new sources of protein to feed the world's growing human population. People might see these forms of food as unnatural, and feel strange about eating them at first. The question is, will people be able to overcome the 'yuck' factor, and try these alternatives to meat?

We eat, on average, 80 kg of meat per person per year, in Europe, America and Australia. In Africa and parts of Asia, people eat much less meat – around 25 kg per person per year. But diets are changing and the demand for meat is growing. There is a link between money and meat too – the wealthier people become, the more meat they tend to consume. ➜

One very interesting solution to this demand for more meat has been the development of 'cultured' meat. Cultured meat is grown in a laboratory. Cells are taken from the types of animals we use for meat, and then the cells are grown in a laboratory to establish a cell culture. The culture is then put into a bioreactor, where it grows into meat cell mush. Nutrients and vitamins are added to the mush, and it is transformed into muscle cells, and then mechanically assembled into a burger patty, or another recognisable type of 'meat shape'.

For some people, this is a simply marvellous invention. You can eat 'meat' without harming an animal, and you don't have to raise animals, feed them, or deal with their waste products, etc. For others, it is a disgusting thought. They think there's something weird, unnatural and unappetising about the idea of eating a substance grown in a petri dish from an animal cell.

There are costs involved – the laboratory equipment has to be kept very sterile and clean. This is because the cells growing in the culture do not have an immune system, like an animal has, so they can be infected by bacteria. However, scientists argue that this 'clean' meat is the protein of the future, and hope to be able to bring it to your table by 2025.

What do you think? Will we be eating cultured burgers soon? Is 'clean' meat a sustainable way to get protein to many people? Is it meat at all?

Part B

Circle the prepositional phrases.

Underline the present perfect tense.

Highlight the future continuous tense.

Scientists across the world, from Amsterdam to Adelaide, have been hard at work developing new sources of protein to feed the world's growing human population. People might see these forms of food as unnatural, and feel strange about eating them at first. The question is, will people be able to overcome the 'yuck' factor, and try these alternatives to meat?

We eat, on average, 80 kg of meat per person per year, in Europe, America and Australia. In Africa and parts of Asia, people eat much less meat – around 25 kg per person per year. But diets are changing and the demand for meat is growing. There is a link between money and meat too – the wealthier people become, the more meat they tend to consume.

One very interesting solution to this demand for more meat has been the development of 'cultured' meat. Cultured meat is grown in a laboratory. Cells are taken from the types of animals we use for meat, and then the cells are grown in a laboratory to establish a cell culture. The culture is then put into a bioreactor, where it grows into meat cell mush. Nutrients and vitamins are added to the mush, and it is transformed into muscle cells, and then mechanically assembled into a burger patty, or another recognisable type of 'meat shape'.

For some people, this is a simply marvellous invention. You can eat 'meat' without harming an animal, and you don't have to raise animals, feed them, or deal with their waste products, etc. For others, it is a disgusting thought. They think there's something weird, unnatural and unappetising about the idea of eating a substance grown in a petri dish from an animal cell.

There are costs involved – the laboratory equipment has to be kept very sterile and clean. This is because the cells growing in the culture do not have an immune system, like an animal has, so they can be infected by bacteria. However, scientists argue that this 'clean' meat is the protein of the future, and hope to be able to bring it to your table by 2025.

What do you think? Will we be eating cultured burgers soon? Is 'clean' meat a sustainable way to get protein to many people? Is it meat at all?

Technology matters

Fact or opinion?

Exercise 1

Alex and Simon are brothers and they are having a conversation about social media. Decide whether each of their statements is fact or opinion and write this in the right-hand column. Underline the parts of the sentence that tell you whether it is a fact or an opinion.

		Fact or opinion?
Alex	Simon, I think you should get off your phone now. You've been spending too much time on social media.	
Simon	Have I? But I've only been on my phone for the last 20 minutes.	
Alex	Maybe, but spending too much time on your phone is bad for your eyes.	
Simon	Well, tell that to the other 3.5 billion social media users. Research shows that over 90 per cent of social media users use their phones to access social media.	
Alex	Wow! That's a very impressive number! Why do you think so many of us use our phones to access social media?	
Simon	Probably because our phones are always in our hands, aren't they? Anyway, best to keep to a short period of time. Mum will take your phone away if she sees you using it now!	

Adjective or adverb?

Exercise 2

Read the sentences below and fill in the blanks with the correct form of the word in brackets. Decide if each word in brackets is an adjective or adverb, and indicate this by writing 'adjective' or 'adverb' on the dotted line at the end of the sentence.

1 Technology helps us to work more .... (efficient). ....

2 Marika .... (calm) restored her files from her backup drive after her

   computer crashed. ....

3 Technology is advancing so .... (rapid) that I can't keep up with the trends.

   ....

4 Governments in some countries use drones to watch their people .... (close).

....

5 Sita learned how to program software very .... (good).

....

6 I heard a .... (terrible) crash in the computer lab. ....

7 I feel .... (guilt) when I spend all day on my computer.

....

8 Part of my .... (daily) routine includes checking my phone for messages the minute I wake up. ....

9 Sabrina used her phone .... (sneak*) under the blankets.

....

10 My neighbours just bought a state-of-the-art sound system. They like to play music very

.... (loud). ....

*sneak – slip in or use without permission

Adverbs 1

Exercise 3a
Fill in the blanks with an appropriate adverb from the box.

manually	physically	automatically	necessary
currently	extremely	indeed	perfectly

The possibilities that drones offer are .... endless. This is why many countries and governments began calling for the design and development of suitable trials that employ drones to conduct automated inspections in train and road tunnels to detect defects such as cracks or water leakage. Such checks are .... done .... and are .... labour intensive as inspectors have to .... search the tunnels looking for defects. Given the current advancements in drone technology, it is .... possible to program a drone to do a 360-degree mapping of the tunnels, ... detect defects from the video taken and provide their location.

This would not only improve the accuracy of inspections, it would also free up engineers' time, allowing them to focus on analysing the data captured to recommend any
.... repairs needed.

Adverbs 2

Exercise 3b

Add adverbs to the passage below. You may use the words in the box or come up with your own words. You may use each word only once and you may not need all of the words in the box.

sleepily	naturally	accidentally	visually	very	obviously	actually
barely	hardly	brilliantly	overly	beautifully	slowly	globally

I had always disliked .... technical things. My interest in how things worked would .... last five minutes before I would scream 'This is too technical for me!'. My natural inclination was towards the arts. I enjoyed literature for the beauty of the language and artwork, especially for the .... painted images. So .... when my father got a teaching position at the Massachusetts Institute of Technology (MIT) and decided that we were going to live on campus, the first thought that came to my mind was, 'I'm going to get so bored'.

I was wrong. We lived in the university staff accommodation and our neighbours were .... fun to be around. One morning, I .... opened my bedroom window and saw that an entire building had been turned into a game. The building had been 'hacked'. It had been .... done.

Fascinated by what I saw, I decided to explore the campus grounds and .... stumbled into the MIT Media Lab. As I walked .... through the rooms, I realised that I was standing in the centre of a research hub that was paving the way for future technologies of the kind I'd never seen before. The university was inventing things that would have an impact .... and had the potential to change lives.

Intensifiers 1

Exercise 4a

Choose the best intensifier for each sentence and write it in the space provided.

1 Your studies will suffer if you spend .... time on social media.

   a much   **b** too   **c** too much   **d** a lot

2 I got .... bored during the programming class last week.

   a very   **b** too   **c** super   **d** much

3 He wastes .... time watching videos that he can never finish his work.

   a such   **b** so   **c** a lot   **d** so much

4 Technology is advancing .... fast for me to keep up with it.

   a too   **b** really   **c** very   **d** quite

5 When Mike's cat destroyed his computer, he was .... angry.

   a a lot   **b** very   **c** sometimes   **d** such

6 I found it .... difficult to spend the weekend in the forest camp without my smartphone.

   a a lot   **b** much   **c** extremely   **d** such

7 I .... hate it when people don't reply to my messages immediately.

   a sometimes   **b** so   **c** quite   **d** absolutely

8 My father .... loves buying the latest tech gadgets.

   a easily   **b** really   **c** sometimes   **d** completely

9 I had .... a good time video chatting with my friends last night.

   a so   **b** very   **c** extremely   **d** such

10 The electric car is .... more expensive than the traditional petrol powered one.

   a much   **b** too   **c** too much   **d** very

Intensifiers 2

Exercise 4b

Add intensifiers to the sentences below to make the adverbs stronger using the words in the box. You will not need to use all of these words.

completely	really	very	extremely	so	more
too	most	at all	a little	by far	much
a lot	quite	slightly	easily	absolutely	

1 My mother replaced our vacuum cleaner with a .... modern one.

2 The computer labs in school are .... outdated.

3 Artificial intelligence technology is .... advanced now.

4 Living off-grid sounds like .... fun for .... while.

5 I could .... give up my phone and laptop for a week.

6 There was .... no way I could leave my phone at home even for one afternoon.

7 I think technology can be .... harmful at times.

8 The flying drone display was one of the .... interesting things I have seen.

9 We should all try .... harder to use less electricity.

10 Watching my brother get into a shouting match with the smart home assistant was

    .... entertaining.

Contradictions

Exercise 5

Read the passages below. Each passage contains a contradiction. Identify the contradiction in each passage and explain why it is a contradiction.

Passage 1

My parents always told us that using the computer for more than two hours a day would spoil our eyesight. As a result, they never allowed me to play video games on my laptop, or even video call with my friends. Recently, all the schools in my country closed because of a national health crisis. My teachers would hold lessons online, and we would need to use the computer all day to access our lessons and complete our assignments. When my eyes tired after the first four hours, my parents forced me to sit in front of the computer for another four hours to study.

Do you think there is a contradiction in this passage? If you agree, explain why you think so.

....

....

....

....

....

> ## Passage 2
>
> I love the internet. It helps me to stay in touch with my friends and family from all around the world. My friends and I play online games together, and even though we are in different countries, it feels like we are together when we play. Sometimes, the internet reminds me of how alone I am over here. All my friends are so far away, and I feel lonely.

Do you think there is a contradiction in this passage? If you agree, explain why you think so.

....

....

....

....

....

Zero, first and second conditionals

Exercise 6

Part A

Fill in the blanks with the correct form of the words in brackets.

1 If you .... (want) me to, I .... (send) you that email later today.

2 If she .... (want) to talk to me, she .... (call).

3 I .... (finish) the programming of the project tomorrow if I

.... (can) find the time.

4 He .... (lose) weight if he .... (stop) gaming

so much.

5 I .... (buy) a new phone if mine .... (become)

outdated.

Part B

Join the two sentences using the zero, first, or second conditional.

1 I have a time machine. I want to travel back in time.

....

....

2 I feel sick. I will have an e-consultation with my doctor.

....

....

3 My friends are overseas. We speak over video call.

....

....

4 Thieves enter the house. The CCTV cameras will catch them.

....

....

5 I use hydroponic technology. I know how.

....

....

Third conditionals

Exercise 7

Join the following sentences using the third conditional.

1 I didn't restart my computer. It crashed.

....

....

2 Samira bought some flour. She baked a cake.

....

....

3 I missed the bullet train. I was late.

....

....

4 Jason dropped his smartphone. It broke.

....

....

5 I drank coffee at night. I couldn't sleep.

....

....

Complete the following sentences using the third conditional.

6 If I had followed my parent's ....

....

7 I would have gone to the festival if ....

....

8 I wouldn't have overslept if ....

....

9 If you had been more organised ....

....

10 ....

.... you wouldn't have been so stressed at the last minute.

Causative verbs

Exercise 8
Fill in the blank with the appropriate causative verbs.

1 Our teacher .... us use our mobile phones in class after we were done with our work.

2 My mother .... me turn off my computer.

3 My brother .... me go to the IT show with him even though I didn't want to.

4 The school .... all the old projectors replaced with brand new ones.

5 I .... my friends to join me on a virtual tour of the Natural History Museum.

6 I .... my little sister borrow my smartphone sometimes.

7 We .... to program our robot to complete the maze to win the competition.

8 Anita .... her mother to agree to .... her go to space camp.

9 Susanna .... her son recycle the trash.

10 Our teacher .... us submit our assignments via the school portal.

Complete the sentences in ways that make sense. Use causative verbs.

11 My mother makes me ....

12 Our teacher let us ....

13 .... store our files on the cloud.

14 I had my parents ....

15 .... an electronic drum set.

Reading comprehension

Exercise 9

Read the article on page 82 of the Student's Book and then answer the questions below.

1 Why was living off-grid the writer's parents' dream? Give two reasons.

....

....

2 The writer says, 'If only we had known …'. What emotion is the writer expressing here?

....

....

3 What does the writer mean by 'Our lives would have been easier if we had thought about this move before we did it'?

....

....

4 'I had to start a compost bin too'. Circle the causative verb in this sentence.

5 Did the writer want to start a compost bin? How do you know?

....

....

6 The writer says that, in the winter, they 'moved into a proper house for a while'. What does the writer mean by 'proper house'?

....

....

7 Identify two inconsistencies in the passage. Write them down in the table.

What the writer said initially	What the writer said later

8 List three things that the writer learned through living off-grid.

....

....

....

Connectives

Exercise 10

Use connectives to join the two sentences together. Join each pair of sentences using two different connectives. An example has been done for you.

I went for a walk. I finished my work.
- I went for a walk <u>after</u> I finished my work.
- I finished my work <u>before</u> I went for a walk.

1 I had fun in school. I learned a lot.

....

....

2 My phone stopped working. I dropped it in a puddle.

....

....

3 My group did well. We used a new presentation software.

....

....

4 I drank coffee. I stayed up all night.

....

....

5 My project is due today. I haven't finished it.

....

....

6 My mother wants me to attend computer classes. I do not.

....

....

7 Ali went to watch a movie in 3D. It gave him a headache.

....

....

8 Laura backed up her computer. She went to bed.

....

....

9 Joey missed the bus. He was late for school.

....

....

10 Ashwin didn't prepare for the competition. He won the competition.

....

....

6 Instant fame

Dependent prepositions 1

Exercise 1a

Fill in the blanks with an appropriate phrase from the box.

different from	interact with	talk about	connect with	upload to
similar to	focus on	look up	post on	follow on

1   You should try to .... others on social media who have the same interests as you.

2   Influencers attend networking meetings to .... their cause.

3   Why don't you .... library archives online for information on influencers and the different ways they promote their cause?

4   Family members should .... more .... their relatives on WhatsApp to develop better communication.

5   Influencers are .... other social media users because they are trying to promote products, services or opinions.

6   They .... data .... the server everyday.

7   Zoom is .... Skype as they both allow video communication.

8   One can only .... pictures .... Instagram.

9   James's mother warned him to .... his school work instead of gaming online.

10 There are many fans who .... their idols .... SnapChat.

Dependent prepositions 2

Exercise 1b
Fill in the blanks with the appropriate dependent prepositions.

Most people these days manage at least one social media platform to post pictures and share experiences. There are many to .... (choose with / choose from). Although all of them come under 'social media', they are .... (different from / different through) one to the other.

Social media platforms are double-edged swords*. On the one hand, they are .... (used to / used from) share happy stories. On the other, they are .... (looked upon / looked in) as an effective platform to publish fake news and gossip that can be damaging and misleading.

Then, there are those who need others to 'like' their posts. It has been difficult for me to understand the real reason behind the actions of social media enthusiasts. I .... (try with / try to) understand how liking other people's posts is motivating or satisfying to sender and recipient. One reason I can .... (come up / come in) with is that they want to be noticed and this gives them the attention they crave.

However, social media platforms are not without advantages. The far-reaching .... (effects of / effects at) social media and the internet have made reunions of long-lost families, children and relatives possible. Dissemination of information is immediate and reaches millions of people at the same time.

Information on social media will always give people something to .... (talk through / talk about). It allows a little distraction from an otherwise stressful life for some people. It widens the net of friendship for people from different countries to .... (connect with / connect from) each other.

So long as social media platforms .... (focus under / focus on) doing good for all, we should not condemn or criticise them.

* Double-edged sword – something that can have both positive and negative consequences

Dependent prepositions 3

Exercise 2

Fill in the blanks with an appropriate adjective, verb or noun from the box and add an appropriate preposition for each sentence.

depend	connect	interact	look	good
similar	agree	focus	argue	different

1 The team is .... designing platforms for social media.

2 It is difficult for the sisters to .... each other on taking turns to use the laptop to visit their TikTok accounts.

3 All social media platforms are .... each other and are used to communicate in particular ways.

4 There are many ways to .... people online.

5 A few social media platforms are .... each other because they communicate information in the same way, using pictures and narratives.

6 Many teenagers .... social media to communicate their feelings instead of speaking to each other in person.

7 A number of students .... computers and the internet to play online games instead of their school work.

8 How effective is it to .... someone you disagree with online when there is a conflict of opinion?

9 Let us .... online .... the profile of the 8-year-old influencer and his latest achievements.

10 I find that I .... better .... people I don't know through social media platforms.

Question tags 1

Exercise 3

Fill in the blanks with the correct question tags.

1 You did create an account on Instagram, ...?

2 Mateo should try to look for his long-lost friend on Facebook, ...?

3 You didn't post those inappropriate videos online, ...?

4 She has many 'likes' on her social media account, ...?

5 Many people are using TikTok, ...?

6 There isn't any research on that new social media platform I heard about, ...?

7 Communicating through social media platforms is convenient, ...?

8 We do not share similar tastes in social media platforms, ...?

9 You should use a different platform to connect with people online, ...?

10 We have to look at what is being shared online, ...?

Question tags 2

Exercise 4

Fill in the blanks in the dialogue with appropriate phrases or question tags.

Betty: You have seen the latest post that Leon posted online, ...?

Sharon: No, what did he say?

Betty: Something about the new social media platform that was recently published. He had a lot to say about it.

Sharon: Really? Was it good or bad?

Betty: Well, he mentioned that there were no privacy settings and it was so poorly designed that he was very sure that it won't be widely accepted. It's doomed to failure, he said.

Sharon: Oh dear! It .... sound bad, doesn't it?

Betty: Oh well, someone must have lost a lot of money setting up the platform, ...?

Sharon: Surely there .... some good things about it, ... there? Otherwise, it shouldn't have been created, ...?

Betty: I am not sure. Perhaps we should check it out, ...?

Sharon: We can do this later, ...?

Betty: Yes, we can. What were you planning to do before that?

Sharon: I have to check some things out online for my essay assignment.

Betty: Oh yes. You do have that paper to finish, ...? Would you like some help with that?

Sharon: I wish you could, but you do know the rules, ...? The lecturer made it quite clear that I should do this by myself.

Collective nouns

Exercise 5

Fill in the blanks with the appropriate collective noun from the box.

class	staff	herd	group	panel
board	bunch	flotilla	swarm	pod

1 The .... of warships made their way home after the war.

2 A .... of dolphins swam alongside our sailboat as we approached Australia.

3 The .... of students organised the exhibition about social media platforms.

4 I did not realise I finished the .... of grapes as I was engrossed in the video I was watching online.

5 The principal arranged for a .... meeting of the teachers to talk about using social media at work.

6 We watched a documentary online for our assignment on the habits of a .... of cows.

7 The .... of judges sat in a meeting to decide whether court proceedings should be recorded on video.

8 After watching the online video, does anyone know how a .... of bees reacts when the queen bee is being threatened?

9   Please arrange for the .... of directors to meet online to discuss problems on shipments around the world because of the pandemic.

10 It is never easy to control an angry .... of people in any situation.

Compound nouns

Exercise 6

Match each word in Box A with a word in Box B to form a compound noun, and use this to complete the sentences below.

Box A

Box A				
foot	suit	copy	news	sky
break	left	sound	light	back

Box B				
fast	scrapers	case	ground	right
paper	track	house	note	overs

1   For more information on social media, please read the .... articles that were recently published.

2   We need to make sure we have a good .... before we begin each day.

3   The ships depend on a .... to guide them in the night.

4   We can have the .... for lunch tomorrow as I cooked too much today.

5   The city has amazing .... that can be seen from far away.

6   Please pack your .... with warm clothing for your trip to Finland.

7   The document has a .... condition that prevents us from making a copy for distribution.

8   Please make sure you read the .... at the end of the article for conditions that may apply.

9   Do we know the .... and history of the influencer who is in the news?

10 I love the .... they used for the documentary on TV.

Direct to reported speech 1

Exercise 7a

Convert the sentences in direct speech to reported speech.

1 'Did you start your homework yet?' Antonio's teacher asked Jennifer.

....

....

2 Her sister said, 'I bumped into your best friend at the computer store yesterday.'

....

....

3 'We should go to the neighbour's house to watch YouTube videos,' she said.

....

....

4 He said, 'I found a new social media platform online a few days ago.'

....

....

5 She asked, 'Did you see the pictures on Suki's Instagram?'

....

....

6 Susie said, 'I am not happy about Timo's comment on Facebook.'

....

....

7 'How many social media platforms are there?' she asked.

....

....

8 'You should stop spending so much time online,' his father said.

....

....

9 'I didn't get a chance to check my TikTok account today because my parents confiscated my phone,' Jacinta said.

....

....

10 Mother yelled, 'If you don't stop surfing the internet, I will throw your phone into the bin!'

....

....

Direct to reported speech 2

Exercise 7b

Convert each sentence or question in the dialogue between Tim and Bud into reported speech.

Tim and Bud met and greeted each other at the computer store. They wanted to buy some accessories for their computers.

Tim: What are you intending to get?

....

Bud: I intend to buy a joystick that is easy to use with many advanced features.

....

Tim: Did you research for the best one online?

....

Bud: Yes, I did.

....

Tim: What is it called?

....

Bud: It's the Thrustmaster HOTAS Warthog and it costs a few hundred dollars.

....

Tim: That is expensive!

....

Bud: I just hope I have brought enough money to pay for it.

....

Tim: I have some money with me in case you don't have enough.

....

Bud: That is great and I will pay you back.

....

Space travel

Past perfect tense and past perfect continuous tense 1

Exercise 1a

Fill in the blanks with the past perfect or past perfect continuous tense of the verbs in brackets.

1 She .... (buy) a few books for her expedition into space.

2 The team .... (live) in the spaceship since last year.

3 The astronauts .... (land) safely back on earth.

4 The scientists .... (write) to the president to ask for more funding for space research.

5 They .... (face) many problems with the equipment in the spaceship since it launched from Earth.

6 He .... (manage) to solve the problem before the astronauts became aware of it.

7 The committee .... (try) to finalise the plans for the launch of their new rocket.

8 Management .... (decide) not to send the rocket into space because of technical difficulties.

9 Many people who .... (watch) the documentary of the rocket that exploded shortly after its launch were in tears.

10 The presidents of the two countries .... (argue) for many days about the funding of the space station.

Past perfect tense and past perfect continuous tense 2

Exercise 1b

Fill in the blanks in the passage with the appropriate tense of the word in brackets.

Many people .... (wait) a long time for humans to finally walk on the moon. When NASA .... (announce) that they were sending a team of astronauts on a manned mission to the moon, people the world over .... (excite).

Many hours of training and preparation went into getting a team of astronauts ready to make the dangerous journey. Neil Armstrong and Buzz Aldrin made history in 1969 for being the first men to land on the moon.

Many people .... (discourage) them from making that journey because they .... (believe) they would not return or would get lost in space. In spite of all the doubts, Armstrong and Aldrin .... (take) the opportunity. The trip .... (success) and they returned to Earth as heroes. Armstrong and his team showed that while perilous, the journey into space could be done. They .... (be) right!

Past perfect tense

Exercise 2a

Turn the statements below into questions in the past perfect tense. One example has been done for you.
- Someone had made shapes in the grass in our lawn. (statement)
- Had someone made shapes in the grass in our lawn? (question)

1 She had been making mistakes with data received from the satellite station in space.

....

....

2 They had repaired the faulty valve in the rocket before.

....

....

3 NASA had been training their astronauts all year round.

....

....

4 He had been studying space exploration in university.

....

....

5 They had trained as rocket engineers previously.

....

....

6 He had designed food capsules for astronauts in space.

....

....

7 They had written about UFOs in their blog about extra-terrestrials.

....

....

8 The team had taken a long time to solve the issue of fuel consumption for the rocket.

....

....

9 We had been planning for this launch for months.

....

....

10 The training for astronauts had evolved since 1969.

....

....

Active voice and passive voice in past perfect tense

Exercise 2b

Part A

The sentences below are in the active voice. Convert them into the passive voice using the past perfect tense. An example has been done for you.

● Some of us had believed fake news of a UFO sighting. (active)
● The fake news of a UFO sighting had been believed by some. (passive)

1 He had told them to be punctual on the day of the launch.

....

....

2 Many people had witnessed the disaster of the rocket shortly after the launch.

....

....

3 Few of us had believed in the existence of extra-terrestrials.

....

....

4 We had watched the documentary on extra-terrestrial life in outer space.

....

....

5 The reporter had said that the stories about UFOs are true.

....

....

Part B

The sentences below are in the passive voice. Convert them into the active voice using the past perfect tense. An example has been done for you.

● The rocket had been launched into space by NASA. (passive)
● NASA had launched the rocket into space. (active)

1 The event had been planned by the space team since the last century.

2 The programme to train astronauts had been designed by the trainers to be tough.

3 The rocket had been maintained well by the engineers.

4 The space exploration project had been terminated by the government due to insufficient funding.

5 The space suits for the astronauts had been designed by scientists to protect them from the cold.

Active voice to passive voice

Exercise 3a

The sentences below are in the active voice. Convert them into the passive voice.

1 Astronauts wear special suits to protect them in space.

2 It takes NASA a long time to train people for space travel.

3 Astronauts use spaceships to travel to space.

....

....

4 They build spaceships to withstand the harsh environment in outer space.

....

....

5 Space explorers know the dangers of spending long periods in outer space.

....

....

6 Many people enjoy watching the launching of rockets into space.

....

....

7 A special group of people carries out space exploration.

....

....

8 Space debris often damages rockets.

....

....

9 Many people admire astronauts and their feat to explore the universe.

....

....

10 Channel 10 news televised the rocket launch.

....

....

Passive voice to active voice

Exercise 3b

The sentences below are in the passive voice. Convert them into the active voice.

1 The spaceship is managed by experienced astronauts.

....

....

2 Extra-terrestrial life is defined by scientists as life found on other planets in outer space.

....

....

3 The spacesuits for astronauts are specially made by manufacturers to withstand the impact of space debris.

....

....

4 The launch of the modern spaceship was watched by millions of people around the world.

....

....

5 The space exhibition event was covered by TV reporters from many countries.

....

....

6 Special training is given by NASA to prepare astronauts for life in outer space.

....

....

7 Signals are sent to Earth by the space station that is in outer space.

....

....

8 Many space expeditions had been carried out by NASA since the last century.

....

....

9 Daily reports are completed by astronauts while they are in space.

....

....

10 Clear verbal communication is received by astronauts from the space research centre on Earth.

....

....

Comprehension

Exercise 4

Read the passage 'Missions to Mars' on pages 112–13 of the Student's Book and answer the questions below.

1 The Rover Curiosity, which has been placed on Mars, sends interesting information back to Earth. Why do you think NASA is looking for information about Mars?

....

....

....

2 Describe two things that have been discovered on Mars so far.

....

....

....

3 What is Elon Musk worried about?

....

....

....

4 Do you think he should spend his money to help fix Earth's problems instead? Explain why.

....

....

....

Relative clauses 1

Exercise 5a

Underline the relative clauses in the sentences below.

1 The training centre, which conducts space programmes, has been running since the 1900s.

2 Astronauts, who studied aeronautical engineering, are specialised and qualified to travel into outer space.

3 Many people who watched the launch of Apollo 13 remember the event today.

4 Mandy goes to the university, where she does aeronautical studies on weekends.

5 Richard visits the museum, which has displays of space history and modern developments, every week.

6 They were looking forward to visiting the aerospace exhibition, which shows how space suits have changed over the years.

7 Many people who are interested in space exploration enjoy witnessing the launch of rockets into space.

8 UFO sightings, which scare people, is a popular topic.

9 A Rover that collects information for NASA has been on Mars for a few years.

10 Asteroid collisions, which can destroy Earth, have happened in outer space.

Relative clauses 2

Exercise 5b
Fill in the blanks with your own words to ensure that the sentences make sense.

1 The fans, ..., greeted the
heroes after their rocket returned to Earth.

2 NASA officials, ..., are trying
to obtain more information about Mars.

3 Many people, ..., hope for the
safe return of their country's astronauts from outer space.

4 The man, ..., likes to look at
the planets through his telescope.

5 The high-powered telescope, ...,
has modern features that allow you to see Saturn.

6 The model rocket, ..., was
very realistic..

7 The police arrested the man, ...,
for getting too close to the launch site.

8 The astronaut, ..., continued
signing autographs for his fans.

9 The photographer, ..., nearly
dropped one of his cameras while trying to take pictures of the flames from the take-off.

10 My mother's house, ..., has
cracked tiles from the vibrations of the rocket taking off.

Relative pronouns

Exercise 6

Fill in the blanks with the appropriate pronoun from the options given in brackets.

1 Neil Armstrong and Buzz Aldrin were the first men .... (who / whom) landed on the moon in 1969.

2 The rocket, ... (which / whose) has modern facilities, will help astronauts return safely to Earth.

3 Space exploration began in the twentieth century when the team, ... (who / which) had government support, wanted to send astronauts to explore planets near Earth.

4 The engineers .... (which / who) built the spaceship found many problems with the spare parts they had to use.

5 They are sure .... (which / that) people can live on Mars.

6 Very few people .... (who / which) have a lot of money can finance an expedition into space.

7 Rockets have spaces .... (who / that) are usually compact.

8 The satellite, ... (which / who) was installed in outer space, needs regular maintenance for it to work well.

9 The children, ... (which / who) were watching the launch of the rocket, screamed with excitement when it took off.

10 I live in an area .... (who / that) is close to the building where scientists conduct research into space exploration.

8 Rules protect us ... don't they?

Simple past tense passive

Exercise 1a

Convert these active sentences into the passive voice using the simple past tense.

1 The president changed the laws on speeding in his country.

....

....

2 One school in this district removed detention as a form of punishment.

....

....

3 The town council imposed a hefty fine on the parkour athletes.

....

....

4 Too many students broke the rule of standing up to greet the teacher in class.

....

....

5 My mother made the rule that we cannot eat in our bedrooms.

....

....

6 She repeatedly disobeyed school rules.

....

....

7 The president selected the country's lawmakers from a list of experienced judges.

....

....

8 The principal addressed the students about new rules for the school.

....

....

9 The town council changed the penalty for illegal parking.

....

....

10 The CCTV recorded the incident of parkour in the shopping mall.

....

....

Simple past tense active

Exercise 1b

Change the verb in brackets into the past tense and rewrite the sentences in the active voice.

1 The rules that were .... (create) by management for latecomers are unfair.

....

....

2 Many people were .... (catch) and .... (fine) by the town council for littering in the neighbourhood.

....

....

3 A few students were .... (punish) by the headteacher for breaking a classroom window.

....

....

4 The vandals were .... (sentence) to community work by the judge for defacing the walls of Parliament House.

....

....

5 A few patrons were .... (ask) to leave the cinema by the ushers for not switching their mobile phones to silent mode.

....

....

6 The shopping mall roof was .... (climb) on by a group of roof-toppers.

....

....

7 Some rules were .... (make) by the building owners with fines to dissuade parkour athletes from roof-topping.

....

....

8 Many things were .... (consider) by the lawmakers before deciding on a deterrent.

....

....

Used to

Exercise 2

Tick to indicate whether the phrase 'used to' is used as an adjective or a verb.

	Adjective (✔)	Verb (✔)
1 I used to participate in school debates when I was younger.		
2 They are used to being asked not to do parkour on public buildings.		
3 We are used to long hours in the office when there is a lot of work to be done.		
4 People used to be treated unfairly in this country.		
5 I am used to the littering problem in my neighbourhood although there are rules against it.		
6 None of the students are used to the school rule of receiving a detention if they do not iron their school uniform.		
7 Karim is used to copying his classmate's homework, although Karim knows it is against school rules.		
8 The school used to issue detentions as a form of punishment, but they have stopped.		
9 The president used to review the laws of the country each year but that does not happen anymore.		
10 We were used to wearing a tie with our uniform in those days and we would be punished if we forgot to bring it.		

Active versus passive

Exercise 3

Tick to indicate which of these sentences are active and which are passive.

	Active (✔)	Passive (✔)
1 The government made sure that the laws were fair but firm.		
2 School rules will be updated from time to time by the school leaders.		
3 Detention will be given by the school for anyone who breaks any of the rules.		
4 The headteacher has students doing detention at least three times a week.		
5 We must be mindful of the environmental laws and rules of the countries we visit.		
6 Often, public property is damaged by visiting tourists who do not have respect for the laws of the country.		
7 Citizens are outraged at tourists from neighbouring countries who persist in breaking environmental laws.		
8 Fines will be imposed by the town council if visitors to the housing estate flout the rules of keeping the vicinity clean.		
9 Do not infringe or break any of the rules by parking illegally when you visit your uncle in the next town.		
10 Be prepared to be punished by the authorities if rules are broken.		

Comprehension

Exercise 4

Part A

Read the article 'Will pangolins be saved?' on page 128 of the Student's Book, then answer the questions below.

1 Why are pangolins being exploited?

....

....

2 What does the word 'endangered' mean? What will eventually happen if pangolins continue to be hunted and killed?

....

....

....

3 Why do you think pangolins are still being trapped and killed?

....

....

....

4 What is one way that pangolins are being protected?

....

....

....

5 In your opinion, are the new laws going to stop the illegal trade of these animals?

....

....

....

Part B

Now read the article 'Roof-Topping Rule-Breakers!' on page 129 of the Student's Book and answer the questions below.

1 Name two rules the parkour athletes are breaking, according to building owners.

....

....

....

2 Knowing that they risk damaging buildings, why do people still do it?

....

....

....

3 Why do the roof-toppers disagree with the building owners?

....

....

....

4 What is your view about what the roof-toppers are doing?

....

....

....

5 Which text did you enjoy reading more? Give two reasons to support your opinion and explain why.

....

....

....

Present continuous tense

Exercise 5
Fill in each blank with an appropriate present continuous tense.

1 I .... to visit an old school friend at the weekend.

2 The principal .... to the whole school about the punishment for arriving late.

3 Students .... continually .... the rule by not ironing their uniforms.

4 They .... not .... school rules and are always late for school.

5 Many people .... to the meeting about the new designs for school uniform.

6 The president .... to convince everyone that changes in the law are good for the country's growth.

7 The lawyers .... him against the accusation that he has damaged a building when doing parkour.

8 The PE teacher .... him to run around the sports field as a punishment for trying to cheat in the running race.

9 I .... an officer at the town council today to ask for a parking permit.

10 The panel of students .... the best suggestions for the end-of-term celebrations.

Present continuous passive 1

Exercise 6a
Rewrite the following sentences using the present continuous passive tense.

1 He is writing a new law to penalise tourists who destroy the country's beaches.

....

....

2 The roof-toppers are training hard to master extreme parkour skills.

....

....

3 The headteacher is implementing detention for school bullies.

....

....

4 The town council is imposing a large fine on visitors who destroy public property of the newly set-up town.

....

....

5 Many people are protesting about fines for illegal parking.

....

....

6 The principal is issuing an order to punish students who do not wear a tie to school.

....

....

7 The management is not allowing clients to use the parking lots designated for their staff members.

....

....

8 The school is implementing new school rules to minimise offences by their students.

....

....

9 The cinema is recommending that patrons leave if they do not put their phones in silent mode.

....

....

10 The bakery is requesting that their customers sanitise their hands before they reach the counter to order.

....

....

Present continuous passive 2

Exercise 6b
Fill in the blanks with the present continuous passive tense using the verb in brackets.

1 Citizens .... (teach) how to understand the rules correctly.

2 Many of the citizens .... (convince) that the new laws will benefit them.

3 Too many students .... (punish) for coming late to school.

4 He .... (issue) with a parking fine for overstaying without paying.

5 They .... (instruct) how to pay the fine by using the machine.

6 .... they .... (stop) from climbing on the roof?

7 .... she .... (tell) to stop videoing the building?

8 A few students .... (see) as rule-breakers.

9 The rules .... (review) to see if changes should be made.

10 We .... (question) by the headteacher for something we did not do.

Connecting words

Exercise 7

Fill in each blank with an appropriate connecting word or phrase from the box.

since	despite	although	however	because of
furthermore	on the other hand	even though	whereas	moreover

1 .... he broke the rules, he was not punished.

2 It is dangerous to text while driving, ..., it is illegal in some countries.

3 He has been working overseas .... his daughter was born two years ago.

4 The citizens are proud of their country's progress with the new laws, ..., they cannot forget the difficulties caused by the old laws.

5 The children were not allowed to leave the house, ..., they were not allowed to open the windows.

6 Pangolins continue to be hunted and killed .... the new laws to protect them.

7 On the one hand, I agree that students who cheat in exams should automatically fail. .... I feel that they should be given another chance to retake the exam.

8 .... the president cares for the citizens in general, he never encouraged people to break the rules.

9 The fines for a late return of a library book were made more expensive .... repeated late returns.

10 All my brothers are lawyers with the government, ... I am a counsellor.

Connectives – unlike or despite?

Exercise 8

Fill in the blanks with either 'unlike' or 'despite'.

1 Understanding the legal system in this country is my favourite topic, ... my sister who prefers to read about wildlife.

2 My family and I are on our way to the festival .... the bad weather.

3 .... implementing new laws to save and protect pangolins, they continue to be hunted and killed for their meat and scales.

4 David is often in trouble for being rude to teachers, ... his brother Tom, who is kind and gentle.

5 Many city-dwellers abide by the laws of the city, ... those from the countryside who are not used to strict laws.

6 .... her fear of breaking the law, Jennifer continued doing extreme parkour.

7 The principal was not hard on students in her school .... the seriousness of the damage to the school window.

8 We prefer to watch the news on television .... others who prefer to read about it in the newspapers.

9 .... my parents, I understand why the roof-toppers enjoy leaping about on buildings.

10 .... not having done anything wrong, I was called to the principal's office.

Comprehension

Exercise 9

Read the article 'The rules you may not even know exist!' on page 132 of the Student's Book, then answer the questions below.

1 Why should there be rules?

....

....

....

2 What do you think might happen if you do not know the rules in a country you are visiting?

....

....

....

3 What is one rule that many schools have?

....

....

....

4 What do you think a 'neighbourhood charter' means?

....

....

....

5 Choose one of the rules from the neighbourhood charter. What might happen if this rule was broken?

....

....

....

6 We sometimes hear people say that 'this is an unwritten rule'. What do you think this implies about this type of rule?

....

....

....

....

....

Dreams and ambitions

Present and past perfect continuous tense

Exercise 1

Fill in the blanks with the correct tense from the box.

has been	have been	had been

1 The five brothers .... singing professionally before they became teenagers.

2 Magic Johnson .... playing professional basketball for thirteen years.

3 This charitable organisation .... donating millions of dollars each year to support victims of natural disasters.

4 She .... dreaming of becoming an actress before she was a professional singer.

5 Leonardo DiCaprio .... running his own charity foundation for the past few years.

6 Amy .... painting before she was three years old.

7 Many of the volunteers .... raising funds for the poor in war-torn countries for years now.

8 Shafiq .... talking about his participation at the protest march for weeks.

9 The twin girls .... attending dance lessons after they watched a ballet performance.

10 Steven Spielberg .... directing movies since 1974.

Compound nouns 1

Exercise 2a

Draw a line from the words in column A to the correct words in column B to create compound nouns.

	A
1	copy
2	sound
3	bill
4	spot
5	suit
6	key
7	screen
8	letter
9	man
10	back

B
hunt
light
case
right
proof
board
note
play
ground
head

Compound nouns 2

Exercise 2b

Complete the blanks in the sentences using a compound noun from the box. You may use a dictionary or search online for the meanings of the words.

foresight	slapstick	newscaster	standout	sideburns
handbooks	spotlight	bodyguard	backstage	comeback

1 The actor is recognised everywhere for his thick .... on either side of his face.

2 The volunteers bring all the props from .... to put into position before the play.

3 He had the .... to enrol his son, who later became a famous actor, into an acting school before he was six years old.

4 The famous singer always had a .... to protect him everywhere he went.

5 She is the only .... in the radio station who reads the headlines from behind a screen.

6 The school gave out .... to people who enrolled.

7 Jade loved being the centre of attention and as a famous actress she knew she would always be in the ....

8 All the applicants were good but not good enough to be a .... success.

9 She made an impressive .... after taking a break for a couple of years.

10 Charlie Chaplin was famous for his .... comedy in silent movies.

Abstract nouns I

Exercise 3a

Fill in the blanks with the appropriate noun in brackets.

1 It takes hard work and a lot of .... (love / determination) to become famous.

2 To have .... (integrity / knowledge) means to be honest and sincere with everyone you deal with.

3 It is sometimes difficult to keep a .... (loyalty / promise) without breaking it.

4 One of Oprah Winfrey's best qualities is her .... (anxiety / honesty).

5 An honourable quality of a genuine friend is .... (embarrassment / loyalty).

6 Audrey Hepburn had a lot of .... (compassion / beauty) as an ambassador for UNICEF.

7 Many young actors show a lot of .... (bravery / enthusiasm) when they first start out because they want to impress and make a name for themselves.

8 Leonardo's .... (selfishness / generosity) with his time and money to save the environment is commendable.

9 It takes a lot of .... (anger / patience) to work with fussy and demanding celebrities.

10 The audience laughed heartily at the comedian's brand of .... (hope / humour).

Abstract nouns 2

Exercise 3b

Complete the blanks in the sentences using an abstract noun from the box. You may use a dictionary or search online for the meanings of the words.

bravery	tribute	success	faith
knowledge	pride	passion	brilliance
honesty	beauty	skill	duty

1 They say you can gain .... when you read widely.

2 His work had that touch of ...., which resulted in him winning an Academy Award.

3 She takes great .... in doing the best work that she can.

4 They have a strong sense of .... and always do whatever it takes to get the job done.

5 Milo received a medal for his act of .... when he saved a baby from a burning house.

6 The concert was a .... to the actor for his charitable work.

7 Have a little .... that things will work out for the best.

8 A great actor takes years of work to master the .... of acting well.

9 .... is the best policy.

10 He has a great .... for acting and singing which has made him one of the most famous celebrities in the world.

Pronouns 1

Exercise 4a

Fill in the blanks with an appropriate pronoun from those in brackets.

1 .... (Everyone / Someone) you know will be at your celebration party.

2 The dresses for the singer are hanging on .... (that / this) rack over there.

3 Will there be .... (anyone / something) at home this afternoon to receive the package?

4 .... (This / Those) are the statuettes for the winners at the Actor's Guild Award ceremony tonight.

5 I would like to know where I should place .... (this / those) bouquet of roses.

6 There is still .... (some / few) fruit punch left from the party.

7 I have .... (this / these) dreams of becoming a writer like J. K. Rowling.

8 My ambition is to act in .... (a few / none) movies by the time I reach 50 years old.

9 It is better to achieve only .... (some / one) dream than none at all.

10 Is .... (all / anyone) keen on getting up early every morning to train?

Pronouns 2

Exercise 4b
Fill in the blanks with the appropriate pronoun in brackets (demonstrative, indefinite or quantitative) to complete the passage.

It takes a lot of hard work to turn your dreams into reality. For those in show business, it takes .... (some / many) years to master the art of acting. For others, they have a natural talent for it. For .... (this / these) actors, they may not have to try so hard to master the art. .... (Little / A few) of them are children of accomplished actors and they learn the art of acting indirectly from their parents.

Hollywood acknowledges the great actors with awards such as the Academy Awards, Actor's Guild Awards, BAFTA Film Awards, Golden Globe Awards, to name just a .... (many / few).

Amateur actors have to take acting lessons in specialised schools. .... (One / Many) famous acting school in the UK is the Guildhall School of Music and Drama, a prestigious drama school. If you are looking for famous acting schools in the US, ... (some / two) of the most famous are Yale and Juilliard.

Editing

Exercise 5

The following story about two friends has spelling and punctuation errors, and incorrect tenses and nouns. Identify the errors and rewrite the story with corrections in the space below.

mark and trina have been friends since they are children they has many things in common they like to ride horses cycle jog and skydive everyone thinks that they will be in each others lives forever it didnt turn out that way when trina leaves her hometown to go to university in another state mark was sad they lost contact with each other for four years

then one day they bumped into each other again and this was how their conversation went

mark: trina is that you

trina: my goodness its been so long how have you been

mark: ive been ok how about you

trina: ive been great i have missed hanging out with you

mark: yeah me too

trina: have you moved here

mark: yeah I am working here what about you

trina: me too

mark: we should meet for a coffee soon to catch up shall we exchange phone numbers

trina: yeah sure i shall like that

....

....

....

....

....

....

....

....

....

....

....

....

....

....

....

....

....

Past perfect continuous 1

Exercise 6a

Convert the following sentences to the past perfect continuous active form.

An example is shown below.
- The winning movie had been judged by a panel. (passive)
- A panel had been judging the winning movie. (active)

1 Bad publicity had been received by the actor.

....

....

2 The exhibition had been successfully prepared by the students.

....

....

3 The ideas had been created by the artists.

....

....

4 The chaos had been caused by the film crew shooting the new movie along that street.

....

....

5 My ambitions had been motivated by my mother.

....

....

6 She had been treated well by the film crew.

....

....

7 Mother had been praised by many people for her humanitarian work.

....

....

8 The crowds had been caused by the celebrities' visit to the city.

....

....

9 Our dreams of becoming musicians had been supported by our parents.

....

....

10 The titles for the movies had been selected by the production team.

....

....

Past perfect continuous 2

Exercise 6b

Convert the following sentences to the past perfect continuous passive form.

An example is shown below.
- The volunteers had been building the ship for celebrities. (active)
- The ship for celebrities had been built by the volunteers. (passive)

1 Many actors had been directing numerous movies.

....

....

2 They had been working on that film for years.

....

....

3 The mother had been shouting at her child.

....

....

4 The family had been searching for the diamond pendant.

....

....

5 The cleaner had been mopping the floor.

....

....

6 My neighbour had been selling his famous beef noodle soup for years.

....

....

7 The drama students had been looking at the Golden Globe Awards for hours.

....

....

8 The nurse had been treating the wound on the girl's leg.

....

....

9 Tammy had been walking that distance to keep herself fit.

....

....

10 Jim had been watching that documentary intently.

....

....

Pronouns and complex noun phrases

Exercise 7

Read the sentences below. Then:

a identify what kind of pronoun has been used (demonstrative, indefinite or quantitative) and write it in the brackets

b underline the complex noun phrases in each sentence.

For example:
● The <u>fat cat</u> has lost some fur. (quantitative)

1 People owning their homes had many complaints because of the new tax. (...................................)

2 Most of his recent successes were those movies that were box office hits. (...................................)

3 All the movie reels are kept locked in this safe. (...................................)

4 Someone who is trying to steal the rare diamonds. (...................................)

5 I like several of the actors in that mystery movie. (......................................)

(......................................)

6 This talk-show host has many antique cars, which are those bought in Europe.

(......................................) (......................................)

7 I am all for the idea of public transportation catering to everyone in this country.

(......................................)

8 That yellow house belongs to the eccentric actor, Dino Falway. (......................................)

9 The strange old man who lives two houses away, owns those parked there.

(......................................) (......................................)

10 We should ask everyone in our tranquil neighbourhood to gather for a party.

(......................................)

Comprehension questions

Exercise 8

Read the article 'Reach for the stars' on page 148 of the Student's Book, then answer the questions below.

1 Write down five facts given about Nancy Roman in this article.

....

....

....

2 What opinion is expressed in the following sentence? *Nancy found it difficult to obtain recognition for her scientific research, but she never gave up?*

....

....

....

3 What was the difference between Nancy's opinion of studying Physics compared to her teacher?

....

....

....

4 Were the ideas expressed by Nancy's teachers based on facts or on their own opinions?

....

....

....

5 Why do you think Nancy found it difficult to obtain recognition for her scientific research at this time?

....

....

....

6 Does Nancy's story inspire you to work in science and technology in the future? Say why, or why not.

....

....

....

The **Cambridge Checkpoint Lower Secondary World English** series consists of a Student's Book, Boost eBook, Workbook and Teacher's Guide with Boost Subscription for each stage.

Student's Book	Boost eBook	Workbook	Teacher's Guide with Boost Subscription
Student's Book 7 9781398311411	eBook 7 9781398307568	Workbook 7 9781398311350	Teacher's Guide 7 9781398307698
Student's Book 8 9781398311428	eBook 8 9781398307599	Workbook 8 9781398311367	Teacher's Guide 8 9781398307704
Student's Book 9 9781398311435	eBook 9 9781398307629	Workbook 9 9781398311404	Teacher's Guide 9 9781398307711

The answers are **FREE** to download from:
www.hoddereducation.com/cambridgeextras

To explore the entire series,
visit **www.hoddereducation.com/cambridge-checkpoint-World-English**

Cambridge Checkpoint Lower Secondary World English Teacher's Guide with Boost Subscription

Created with teachers and students in schools across the globe, Boost is the next generation in digital learning for schools, bringing quality content and new technology together in one interactive website.

The **Cambridge Checkpoint Lower Secondary World English Teacher's Guide** includes a print handbook and a subscription to Boost, where you will find a range of online resources to support your teaching.

- **Confidently deliver the new curriculum framework:** Coverage of framework learning objectives are included along with an interactive Scheme of Work, starter suggestions, activity guidance and notes on differentiation and formative assessment.

- **Develop key concepts and skills:** Let students see how their skills are developing with knowledge tests and worksheets.

- **Enrich learning:** Images from the Student's Book to be used front of class, audio recordings plus transcripts and vocabulary flashcards.

To purchase Cambridge Checkpoint Lower Secondary World English Teacher's Guide with Boost Subscription, visit www.hoddereducation.com/ cambridge-checkpoint-World-English

Cambridge checkpoint

Lower Secondary World English WORKBOOK

9

Support knowledge and understanding from the Student's Book with this practical workbook designed to challenge students to develop their learning further.

- Save time when planning with ready-made homework or extension exercises.
- Ensure mastery with clear coverage of key language skills: reading, writing, speaking, listening and use of English.
- Develop and expand knowledge, ensuring learners master the skills, language systems and vocabulary from every unit.

For more information on how to use this workbook, please visit: **www.hoddereducation.com/workbook-info**

For over 25 years we have been trusted by Cambridge schools around the world to provide quality support for teaching and learning. For this reason we have been selected by Cambridge Assessment International Education as an official publisher of endorsed material for their syllabuses.

Working for over
25 YEARS WITH
Cambridge Assessment International Education

This resource is endorsed by Cambridge Assessment International Education

- ✓ Provides learner support as part of a set of resources for the Cambridge Lower Secondary English as a Second Language curriculum framework (0876) from 2020
- ✓ Has passed Cambridge International's rigorous quality-assurance process
- ✓ Developed by subject experts
- ✓ For Cambridge schools worldwide

Boost
This series includes eBooks and teacher support.
Visit www.hoddereducation.com/boost for more information.

Registered Cambridge International Schools benefit from high-quality programmes, assessments and a wide range of support so that teachers can effectively deliver Cambridge Lower Secondary.

Visit **www.cambridgeinternational.org/ lowersecondary** to find out more.

HODDER EDUCATION
e: education@hachette.co.uk
w: hoddereducation.com

ISBN 978-1-398-31140-4

9 781398 311404

MIX
Paper from responsible sources
FSC™ C104740